I AM A DRAGON

THIS COLORING BOOK BELONGS TO:

____

____

Color Test Page

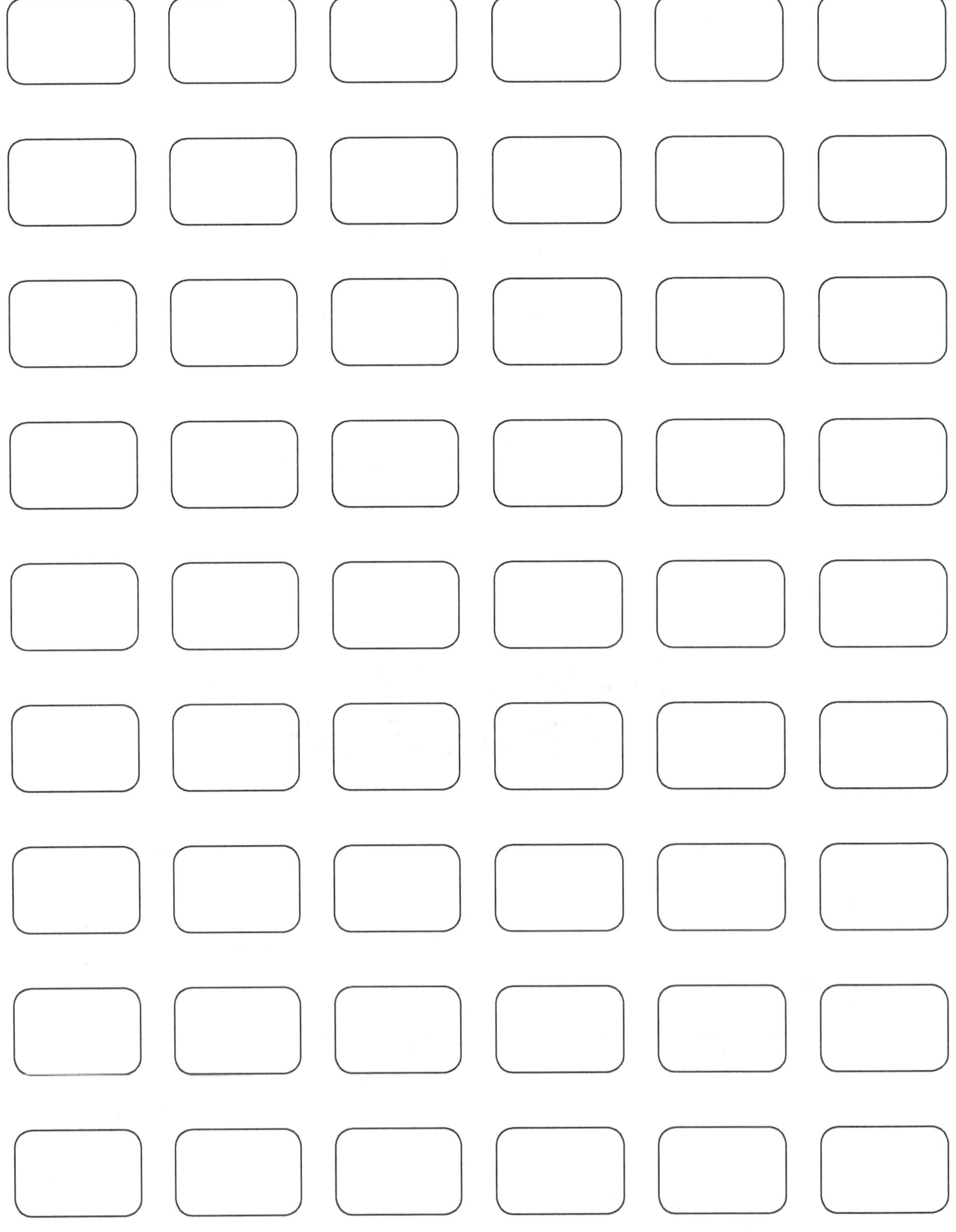

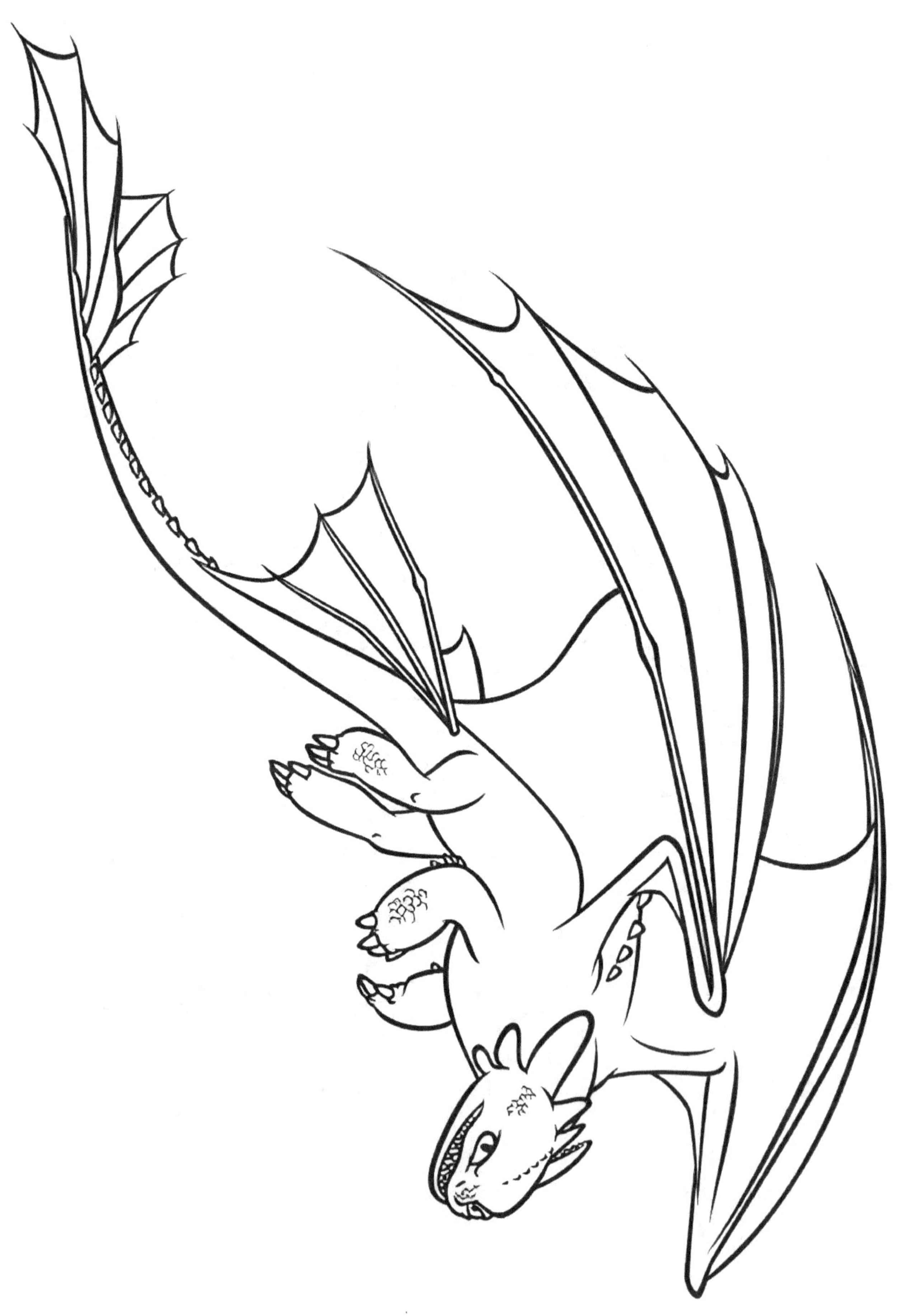

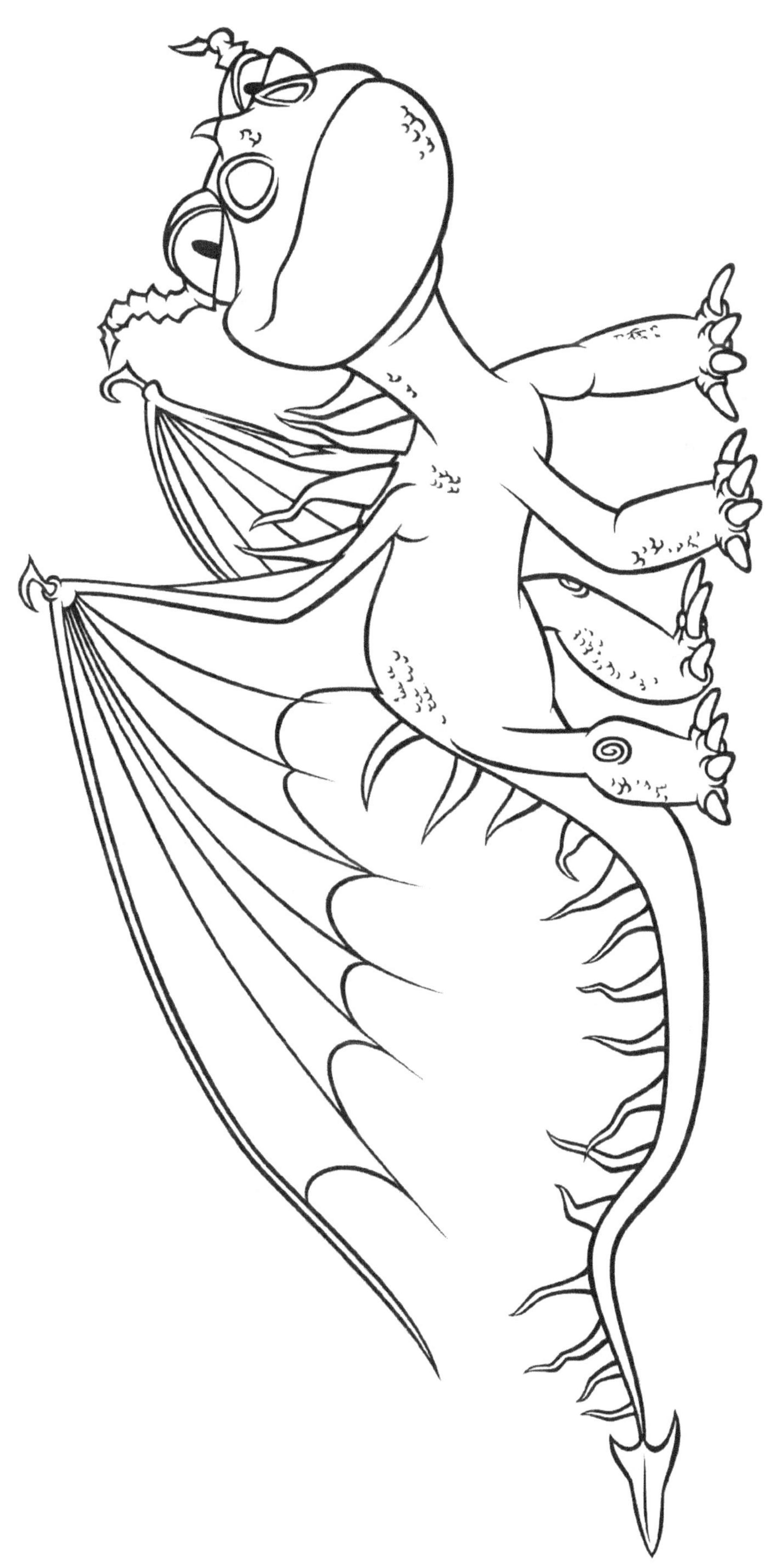

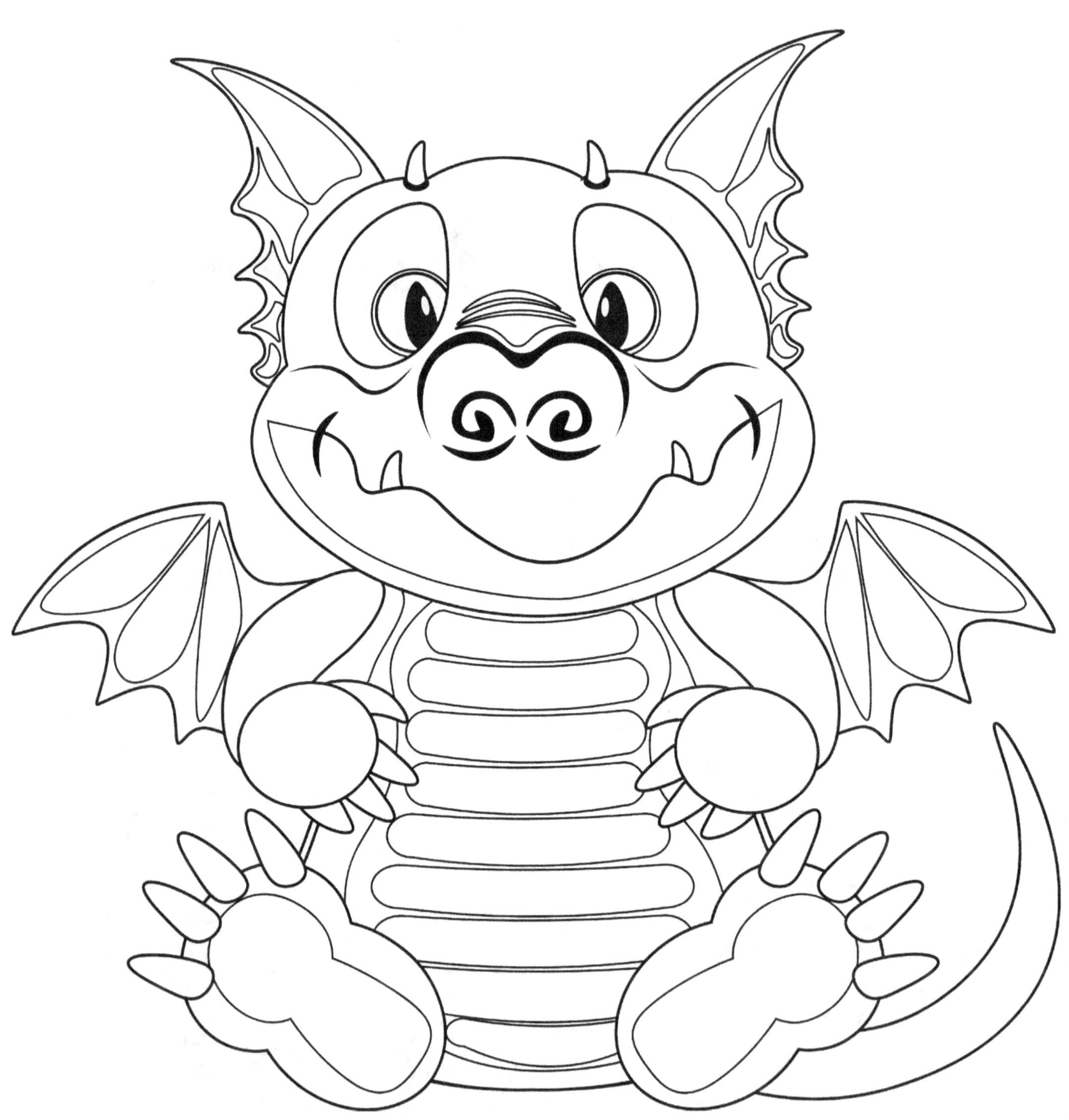

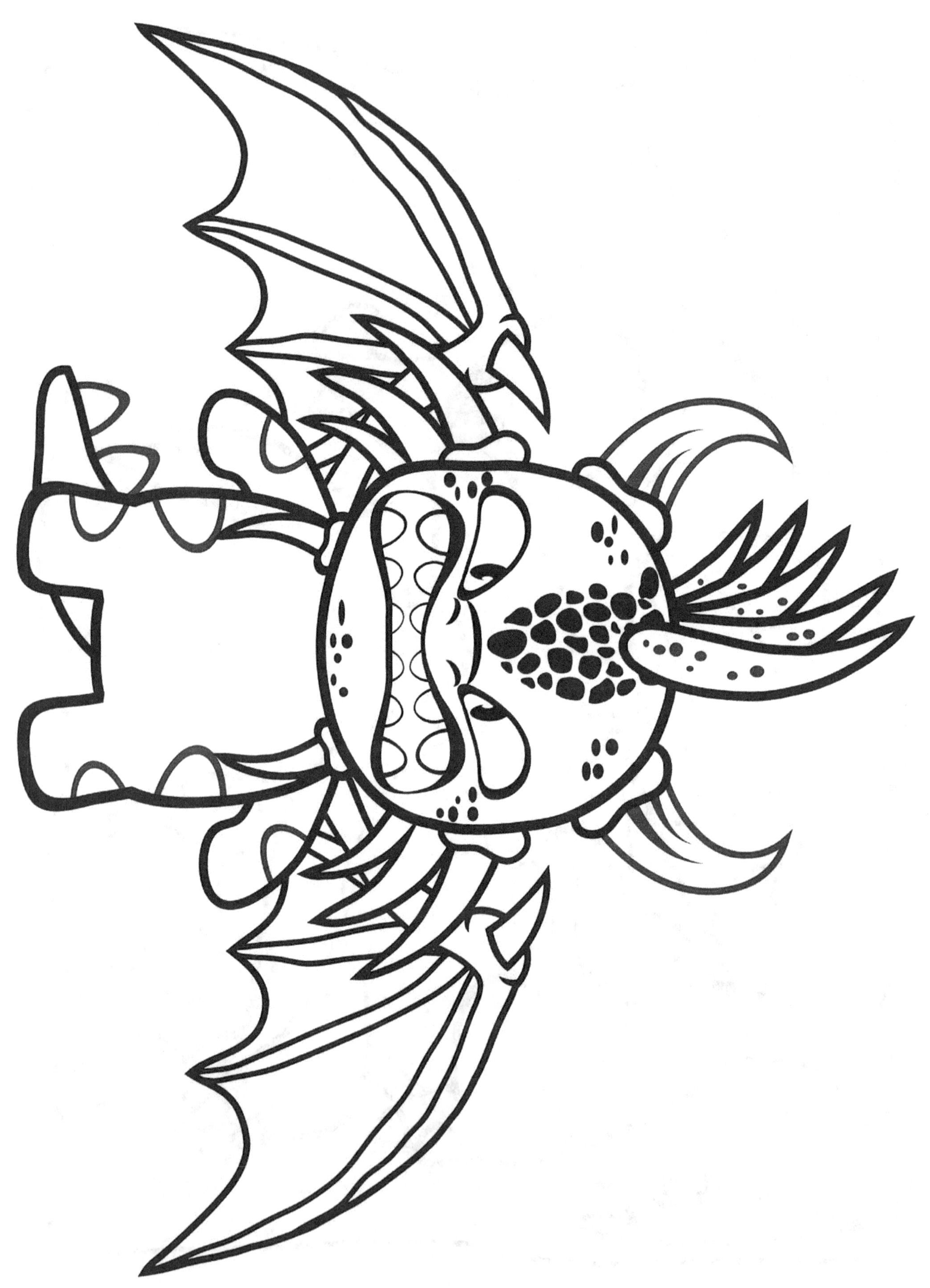

I AM A
DRAGON